Family Retreat for First Eucharist

The Eucharist is who we are—each and every day. It's not just about *First* Communion, as important as that is. Eucharist is about the weekly celebration of the liturgy for the rest of our lives, and how we live the Eucharist each day of our lives.

The preparation and ongoing understanding of Eucharist (and all the sacraments) is not just for the children; this sacred time of preparation touches and affects the entire family. The opportunity for a retreat helps families not only prepare for *First* Communion but understand and appreciate every Communion throughout our lives.

How to Use this Resource

There is much, much more in this resource than you could ever use in one retreat. Several ideas for activity centers are given so that you can choose which would be most helpful for your families. And/or—you might use all of them in designing and hosting three retreats for families throughout the year...or even one after the celebration of First Communion (reminding people that our learning and appreciation of the sacrament never ends).

One activity center ("The Gift of the Holy Spirit") is designed for parishes that are celebrating the restored order of the sacraments.

In addition to the various activity centers, there is also:

- a full-group beginning activity that culminates in a simple soup and bread lunch (dinner) at the end;
- a full-group closing activity that could precede the soup and bread lunch (dinner).

TWENTY-THIRD PUBLICATIONS, a Division of Bayard, Inc.
One Montauk Avenue, Suite 200; New London, CT 06320 • (860) 437-3012 or (800) 321-0411 • www.twentythirdpublications.com

ISBN: 978-1-62785-544-0 • Cover and text illustrations: ©Shutterstock.com • Printed in the U.S.A.

Depending upon how you design your time, it might not be possible to use both the beginning activity and closing activity. Pick and choose, or use one at one time, the second at another time.

All of these activities are designed to be continued at home. A mother once told me, "I want to pray at home; I want to talk about God at home, but I don't know where to start." These activities—begun at the parish and continued at home—show the way.

Preparation

PRELIMINARY PREPARATIONS

- ☐ Read through this resource. Choose the activities that will be most helpful for your families.
- ☐ Schedule the time and place for this family retreat, reserving the necessary space(s) on the parish calendar.
- ☐ Design a flyer/registration form to publicize the gathering to all families (see "Communicating with Families," page 4).
- ☐ Gather and prepare the materials needed.

SPACES NEEDED

- One large room (with tables and chairs) for the opening and closing activities (near a kitchen).
- Several rooms or spaces within a large room (with tables and chairs) for the number of small group activities/ stations that you decide to use (e.g., if each family is going to have the opportunity to move around to three different activities, you will need three rooms (or three spaces within a large room).
- If the "What do I see at church?" activity is one of your choices, families will need to have access to the church.

STAFF

- A catechetical leader is needed to lead the families through the welcome and directions for the movement to the different locations/activities and the opening and closing activities.
- It would be helpful to have catechists/ catechetical leaders available in/near each activity center to answer questions, offer help, and provide encouragement to the families.
- A hospitality team of three or four people can assist in welcoming the families and overseeing the simple lunch of soup and bread (if you choose to do the opening activity).

RETREAT SCHEDULE

As you read through this entire resource, you will see that each parish's schedule might be very different. There are multiple possibilities of activities. Choose those that are best for your families, your timing, and your spaces. You might use:

- The full-group opening and closing activities (without any family-group activities).

- The opening and closing activities with time for two or three family activities.
- The opening activity and family activities (and not the closing activity).
- Two or three family activities and the closing activity

There are also several different ways to bring the retreat to a close. See page 10 for some possibilities.

MATERIALS

Name tags If you choose three activities, divide your families into three groups. As you make their name tags, 1/3 are made in one color; 1/3 are made in a second color; 1/3 are made in a third color. (If you are using two activities, divide your families into two groups.)

Agenda Using card stock or a half sheet of paper, prepare an agenda to give to the families with their name tags. (Depending on what you decide to do, your schedule could look different.)

9:15 AM Prayer and Opening Activity
Room _________

10:00 – 10:20 AM
Yellow Group – Room (or station) #1
Blue Group – Room (or station) #2
Green Group – Room (or station) #3

10:25 – 10:45 AM
Blue Group – Room (or station) #1
Green Group – Room (or station) #2
Yellow Group – Room (or station) #3

10:50 – 11:10 AM
Green Group – Room (or station) #1
Yellow Group – Room (or station) #2
Blue Group – Room (or station) #3

11:15 – 12:00 NOON Closing Activity;
Prayer and Soup: Room __________

Bell or chimes Ring to alert families when it is time to move to the next activity.

Directions sheet When you decide which family activities you will use, you will need copies of the directions sheet (one for each family).

Handouts If the activities you choose to use include handouts, copies will need to be made for each family.

If using the opening activity with its closing lunch: plates, bowls, napkins, silverware, cups, drinks, bread and butter.

If using the opening activity but not having lunch, provide containers for each family to take soup home for a family meal.

Closing activity Assemble materials for the closing activity.

Many other materials are needed for each activity. Be sure to check the list of supplies for each activity you choose to use.

Communicating with Families

In your catechetical schedule for the year, include the date, time, and place for the retreat with a note that the entire family is invited to this day of prayer and learning activities.

☐ *Two months before the retreat:* remind families of the coming date and time.

☐ *One month before the retreat:*

- Remind families of the date and time.
- Ask that they return the registration form within the next ten days.
- If you are using the opening activity: ask them to bring one item for the stone soup. Ask $^{1}/_{6}$ of the families to bring one cup of cut-up carrots; $^{1}/_{6}$ to bring one cup of cut-up celery, $^{1}/_{6}$ to bring one cup of cut-up green beans, $^{1}/_{6}$ to bring one cup of cut-up chicken, $^{1}/_{6}$ to bring one cup of corn, and $^{1}/_{6}$ to bring one cup of noodles.
- If you are using the blessing cup activity, invite them to bring a large wine glass (if they would like), which will be decorated and then used at home to hold prayer cards. (If they don't bring one, you can have some on hand for them.)
- If you are using the "We Listen to God's Word" activity, invite them to bring with them their family Bible.

☐ *Two weeks before the retreat:* check in with the families who have not yet registered.

☐ *One week before the retreat:* remind the families of the date, time, and place, and the things to bring.

An Overview of the Activities and Materials Needed

Opening Activity: The Story of Stone Soup

(and what it tells us about our eucharistic celebration)

PREPARATION

Recruit catechists and/or parents to be the narrator and seven actors

Narrator at microphone

Seven actors can share handheld microphones

SUPPLIES/MATERIALS

Scripts for the narrator and seven actors (*see handouts*)

Card table

"Fire" drawn on large sheet of paper to put around the card table

Large cooking pot

Large spoons to stir

Several pitchers of water

3 large stones (which have been washed and boiled clean)

Hats for soldiers

Chicken broth simmering (in the kitchen)

Soup ladles

After the stone soup is "assembled" during this opening activity, the hospitality committee can add it to the broth and let it simmer until the closing activity. You might also want to add a little bit of onion, a bay leaf, and some spices (such as thyme, pepper, basil, oregano, etc.).

Activities to Choose From

Choose the activities most helpful to your group. There are multiple possibilities of activities. Choose those that are best for your families, your timing, and your spaces.

"What do I see at church?" Activity
(*page 14*)

- ☐ directions sheet for each family
- ☐ As an optional part of this activity, "What do I see at church" cards and stickers are available from Bayardfaithresources.com or 1-800-321-0411 (*order code:* STSA).

We Listen to God's Word Activity
(*page 16*)

- ☐ directions sheet for each family
- ☐ Bibles (provide one for each family, or ask them—in your communication prior to the retreat—to bring their Bibles)
- ☐ large construction paper or poster board
- ☐ pencils
- ☐ crayons/markers

Blessing Cup Activity
(*page 17*)

- ☐ directions sheet for each family
- ☐ a large wine glass for each family, if they are not bringing their own
- ☐ permanent markers
- ☐ stickers, yarn, ribbon
- ☐ small pieces of paper
- ☐ pencils

Our Daily Bread Activity
(*page 18*)

- ☐ directions sheet for each family
- ☐ several patterns of a loaf of bread that families can use for tracing (*see handouts*)
- ☐ white and brown construction paper and/or brown paper bags
- ☐ pencils
- ☐ scissors

We Gather for Meals Activity
(*page 20*)

- ☐ directions sheet for each family
- ☐ Bibles with a bookmark at (or copies of) Luke 22:14–20
- ☐ promise card for each family (*see handouts*)
- ☐ pencils

The Eucharist Is about Making Peace Activity (*page 22*)

- ☐ directions sheet for each family
- ☐ paper to make placemats
- ☐ pencils
- ☐ crayons/markers

We Gather to Give Thanks Activity
(page 23)

- ☐ directions sheet for each family
- ☐ large sheets of construction paper
- ☐ pencils, colored pencils, markers

The Eucharist Commits Us to Action Activity *(page 24)*

- ☐ directions sheet for each family
- ☐ handout for "The Eucharist Commits Us to Action"
- ☐ scissors
- ☐ staplers

My Reflections on Eucharist Activity
(page 26)

- ☐ directions sheet for each family
- ☐ banner kit
  (A ready-made kit, "Individual First Communion Banner," is available from Bayardfaithresources.com or 1-800-321-0411 (*order code:* FCF)
- ☐ scissors

The Gift of the Holy Spirit Activity
(page 27)

- ☐ directions sheet for each family
- ☐ using the handout, cut apart each explanation of the work of the Holy Spirit and place them in a box, a bowl, or a bag (have enough for the number of families who would be in this center at any given time)
- ☐ clay
- ☐ paper to place underneath the clay while working with it

Closing Activity *(page 29)*

- ☐ one hanger for each family
- ☐ an envelope of symbols for each family (*See the handout sheet of symbols*. Make copies and cut them into the shapes ahead of time. Punch a hole at the top of each one.)
- ☐ yarn or ribbon

Simple Closing Lunch (Dinner)

- ☐ stone soup
- ☐ bread and butter
- ☐ drinks
- ☐ plates, bowls, silverware, cups, napkins

Leader's Guide

On the following pages you will find:

- directions and talking points for the day's welcome and prayer, the opening and closing activities, and the closure/closing prayer
- the directions sheets (which will be given to each family) for the possible family activities (These are written for the families; be sure to check the items needed in the preceding list on pages 6-7.)
- the handouts needed for the opening activity, some of the family activities, and the closing activity

Welcome and Prayer

PREPARATION

Choose a leader, reader, and parent for the prayer.

Thank families for their presence, for their faith and their desire to grow together, to deepen their understanding and love for the Eucharist.

Invite families who are near one another to introduce themselves to each other.

Set the day in context. Say something similar to:

- *"You're here today because we are thinking about one of the greatest gifts in our faith: Jesus' presence to us in the sacrament of the Eucharist."*
- *"Moms and dads, several years ago you celebrated the first sacrament with your young child: baptism."*
- *"As we begin today in prayer, let us remember our baptism."*

Leader: Loving God, these parents love their children so much that they continually pray for them: that you will protect them, guiding them from all harm; that you will fill their days with love and joy; that you will help them—as they learn and grow—to always know they are loved.

A parent: Protecting God, because of our love for our children and our desire for you, we brought our children to church to be baptized. United with you, and all your family here and around the world, may we and our children always be friends of Jesus. Amen.

Reader: Many places in Scripture tell us about baptism. We listen to this passage from the Acts of the Apostles: "Once they began to believe Philip as he preached the good news about the kingdom of God and the name of Jesus Christ, men and women alike were baptized." (Acts 8:12)

Leader: On our baptismal days, our parents and godparents, traced on our foreheads the Sign of the Cross, reminding us that we belong to God, that we are followers of Jesus. Moms and dads, take a quiet moment to reverently trace the Sign of the Cross on your child(ren)'s foreheads.

Invite all to pray the Our Father together.

- Continue with the opening activity or, if you are not using it, give directions (referring to the card that they have with their color), of how to proceed to the first family activity.

Opening Activity: Stone Soup and the Eucharist

Invite everyone to think for a moment: *what family meal do you remember most from this past year. Why?*

When you remember that meal, how did everyone help with the preparations and clean-up for that meal?

Is every family meal as special as the one you just thought about? Probably not…

Invite families to talk together for a moment about: *What are some things you can do to make each meal special…less busy…less rushed…more peaceful?*

(If time), invite people to share one of their ideas with the whole group.

Continue by explaining: *We have a story we'd like to share with you about a special meal that occurred once. During our "play" today, the making of a unique soup takes place—and you will have a part in the play.*

Use the script (pages 11-13) and the list of materials needed.

After the story, invite discussions using some of these talking points:

- Ask the whole group:

  What did you like about the story?

  Did you ever go to a dinner that was something like what happened in this story?

- As Catholics, we have a special meal celebration that is sort of like stone soup.

  The Eucharist is not just the priest's job; everyone who is there brings something.

  Some of the things we bring are things all of us bring.

  Some people bring things that others don't (the gift of reading as a lector, etc.)

Invite families to talk for a few minutes, and then hear their ideas (adding to them, if necessary): *What are some of the gifts people in our parish and all of us bring to Mass?* (Our acts of love from the past week; our singing; our prayer; lectors bring their gift of proclaiming God's word…)

After this discussion, give directions for the activity centers and the order in which to move to them. (See suggestions for their agenda card in the materials section; this might differ depending on your timeline.) Remind them that everyone will reconvene at __________.

Other activities you choose take place here.

Closing of the Retreat

Prepare materials for the closing activity. There are several options to close the family retreat:

Option 1 Reassemble as a full group for a simple lunch of bread and soup (the Stone Soup that was made earlier) and a closing prayer (page 32).

Option 2 Reassemble for a full-group closing activity (page 29), followed by soup and bread and closing prayer (page 32).

Option 3 Closing Prayer (page 32) and give each family a container of soup to take home for their family meal.

SCRIPT

The Story of Stone Soup

NEED: *Narrator, First Soldier, Second Soldier, Third Soldier, Paul, Françoise, Albert, Louise*

Narrator: Three soldiers trudged down a road in a strange country. They were on their way home from the war. Besides being tired, they were hungry. In fact, they had eaten nothing for two days.

First Soldier: How I would like a good dinner tonight!

Second Soldier: And a bed to sleep in!

Third Soldier: But all that is impossible. We must march on.

Narrator: On they marched. Suddenly, ahead of them they saw the lights in the village.

First Soldier: Maybe we'll find a bit to eat there.

Second Soldier: And a loft to sleep in.

Third Soldier: No harm in asking.

Narrator: Now the peasants of that place feared strangers. When they heard that three soldiers were coming down the road, they talked among themselves. They said:

Paul, Françoise, Albert, and ***Louise:*** Here come three soldiers. Soldiers are always hungry. But we have little enough food for ourselves.

Narrator: They hurried to hide their food. They pushed sacks of barley under the hay in the lofts. They lowered buckets of milk down the wells. They spread old quilts over the carrot bins. They hid their cabbage and potatoes under the beds. They hung their meat in the cellars. They hid all they had to eat. Then, they waited. The soldiers stopped first at the house of Paul and Françoise.

First Soldier: Good evening to you. Could you spare bit of food for three hungry soldiers?

Narrator: Paul and Françoise made a sad face.

Paul: We have had no food for ourselves for three days.

Françoise: It has been a bad harvest.

Narrator: The three soldiers traveled to the home of Albert and Louise.

First Soldier: Could you spare a bit of food? And do you have some corner where we could sleep for the night?

Albert: Oh no. We gave all we could spare to soldiers who came before you.

Louise: Our beds are full.

Narrator: At Vincent and Marie's the answer was the same. It had been a poor harvest and all the grain must be kept for seed. So it went all through the village. No peasant had any food to share. They all had good reasons. One family had used the grain for feed. Another had an old, sick father to care for. All had too many mouths to fill. The villagers stood in the street and sighed. They looked as hungry as they could. The three soldiers talked together. Then the first soldier called out:

First Soldier: Good people! We are three hungry soldiers in a strange land. We have asked you for food, and you have no food. Well, then, we'll have to make stone soup.

Narrator: The peasants stared. Stone soup? That would be something to know about.

*The **Three Soldiers** gather around a card table.*

Narrator: As the soldiers and the peasants gathered in the village square, the soldiers said:

First Soldier: First we'll need a large iron pot.

***Paul** brings forward a large iron pot.*

Narrator: The soldiers looked at one another and said:

Second Soldier: That's none too large. But it will do and now we need water to fill it and a fire to heat it.

***Paul** and **Françoise** bring forward pitchers of water. The **Three Soldiers** take the pitchers of water and pour the water into the pot.*

Narrator: It took many pitchers of water to fill the pot. A fire was built on the village square and the pot was set to boil.

*The **Three Soldiers** attach the paper fire to the table and mime building a fire.*

Narrator: When the water was boiling, the soldiers said:

Third Soldier: And now, if you please, three round smooth stones.

Narrator: Those were easy to find.

***Albert** and **Louise** bring forward three stones. The **Three Soldiers** place them in the pot.*

Narrator: The peasant's eyes grew round as they watched the soldiers drop the stones into the pot. As the soldiers stirred the stone soup, they said to one another:

First Soldier: Stones like this generally make good soup. But oh, if there were carrots, it would be much better.

*The **Three Soldiers** talk among themselves, such as: "If we only had some carrots… I wonder if anyone in this village has a few carrots they could share with us…" They keep this conversation up until all the children with carrots bring them forward.*

*When all the children bring the carrots forward, the **Three Soldiers** enthusiastically thank them and place the carrots in the pot.*

Narrator: The soldiers continued to make their soup and said to one another:

Second Soldier: A good stone soup should have celery.

*The **Three Soldiers** talk among themselves in the same manner, coaxing everyone to bring forward their celery.*

Narrator: The soldiers looked at one another, smelled the soup, and said:

Third Soldier: This is going to be good soup. You know, it could be even better if we had some green beans.

*The **Three Soldiers** talk together in the same manner until the green beans are brought up.*

Narrator: The soldiers said to one another:

First Soldier: This would make terrific stone chicken soup if only we had some chicken to add to it.

*The **Three Soldiers** again talk among themselves until all bring forward the chicken.*

Narrator: The peasants stared in amazement. A rich person's soup—and all from a few stones. It seemed like magic. The soldiers said to one another:

Second Soldier: If we only had some corn, this soup would be fit for the king himself. Indeed, he asked for such a soup when last he dined with us.

Narrator: The peasants looked at each other. The soldiers entertained the king! Well!

*The **Three Soldiers** talk together, wishing they had corn so they could make the soup like they had made the soup for the king.*

Narrator: As the peasants stared in great wonder, the soldiers said:

Third Soldier: The only thing left would be if we had some noodles!

*The **Three Soldiers** talk and then thank when the noodles are brought forward.*

Narrator: The stone soup was finished! As the soldiers stirred the soup, the delicious smell filled the air. Amazed at what the soldiers did, the peasants stood up and cheered the soldiers.

*Wait for all to stand up and cheer. The **Three Soldiers** then exit.*

Narrator: The soup simmered for a few more hours. When it was time to eat, the peasants set a great table in the middle of the village. As they prepared to eat, they brought from their homes bread, muffins, a roast, and delicious cider to share with one another. It was a celebration they had never seen before—and it all started from three stones!

ACTIVITY

"What do I see at church?"

PARENTS: *You will not be able to visit all these places in church in our short twenty minutes. Begin today and visit whichever ones you'd like—and then continue the others on Sunday mornings after you've celebrated Mass with your parish community.*

If you are using the card and stickers

» Find the place/the item in church.

» Talk together about the explanation on the back of the card.

» After you have completed the suggestion or answered the question below for each one, place your sticker on your card. (If you don't know some of the answers, look them up when you're at home or ask someone on the parish staff.)

Doors

- Why do you think we have churches?
- What do your church doors look like?
- If you were designing a church door, what would it look like?

Baptismal font and holy water fonts

- Was anyone in your family baptized at this baptismal font?
- What's the shape of your baptismal font? What do you think this shape means?
- How many holy water fonts are in your church?
- Slowly pray the Sign of the Cross together. Why do we sign ourselves each time we enter (and leave) church?

Candles

- What is the Paschal candle? When is it used?
- What are the decorations on the Paschal candle?

Prayerful art

- What statues are in your church? Why do you think these were chosen?
- What stories are told in the stained-glass windows?
- Can you find the Stations of the Cross? When, and how, do we pray these?

Vestments

- Can you name the different colors that are used for the vestments? What might each color mean?
- What color is being used right now?

Hymnals and missal

- What is your favorite hymn to be sung at church?
- Can you find a hymn in the hymnal that you don't know but would like to sing?

The Lectionary

- Stand, sit, or kneel near the ambo from which the word of God is proclaimed. Using one of the missals, can you find the readings for next Sunday?
- Read one of the readings. What one word or phrase jumped out at you?
- Pray together:
  May the word we just heard, and will hear again proclaimed on Sunday, live in us; may we be God's word for each other and for our world, this week and always. Amen.

Pews and kneelers

- In addition to pews and kneelers, we also genuflect and bow. We genuflect to the tabernacle, which holds the Body of Christ. We bow to the altar and at the name of Jesus; we bow when we say "*and by the Holy Spirit was incarnate of the Virgin Mary, and became man*" in the Nicene Creed; we bow before receiving the Body of Christ and the Blood of Christ.
- Go to the tabernacle; genuflect in front of it.
- Go to the altar, bow before it.

The altar

- Is this altar similar in any way to your family dinner table?
- God calls us to gather around this dining-table-turned-altar. At Mass, we give God our gifts of bread and wine; God makes them holy, giving them back to us as the Body and Blood of Jesus. Very slowly and reverently, kiss the altar as a sign of respect and gratitude for the gift of Jesus' life.

Bread and wine

- Because we do what Jesus said—"Do this in memory of me"—the bread and wine become the Body and Blood of Jesus.
- Not only are the bread and wine changed, but we are changed. We, too, become the body of Christ in our world.
- What can you do to be the body of Christ to and for all the people you know?

Tabernacle

- Where is the tabernacle in your church?
- Is the sanctuary lamp lit? Why (and when) is it lit?

Crucifix

- Jesus was killed because some people didn't like his teachings. They wanted him to stop, but Jesus couldn't stop teaching and living God's love and God's call to us. How is God asking you to live the teachings of Jesus?
- In some churches, the cross is a resurrected Christ to remind us that Jesus is alive with us and always brings us new life.

Confessionals

- Does your church have confessionals or reconciliation rooms?
- How many are in your church?

ACTIVITY

We Listen to God's Word

PARENTS: *Talk with your family about:*

- God is present with us in many ways. One of them is in **Scripture**—God's word to us.
- At **Mass**, we experience God's presence with us as we listen and respond to God's word.
- The **first reading** is usually from the Old Testament (except during the Easter season when it is from the Acts of Apostles). Take a few minutes to find the Old Testament and the Acts of the Apostles in the Bible.
- The **second reading** is usually from the Letters written by some of the apostles—most often, Saint Paul. During Eastertime, we read from the Book of Revelation. As you look at your Bible, who does Paul write to? Who else wrote some of the letters?
- The **gospel** is our third reading. What are the four gospels?
- After the first reading, everyone prays the **responsorial psalm**. We pray these words, which have been prayed for centuries and centuries. (It would be a wonderful idea to use the response verse from each Sunday in your family prayer during the following week.)
- Listed here are some **response** verses from the psalms. Choose one that your family likes. Letter it on a poster, and decorate it with designs and/or with pictures of what the verse means to each of you.

This is the day the Lord has made; let us rejoice and be glad. **PSALM 118:24**

All the ends of the earth have seen the saving power of God. **PSALM 98:3**

Be with me, Lord, when I am in trouble. **PSALM 91:15**

Lord, send out your Spirit, and renew the face of the earth. **PSALM 104:30**

The Lord is my light and my salvation. **PSALM 27:1**

For you my soul is thirsting, O Lord my God. **PSALM 62:2**

I will walk in the presence of the Lord in the land of the living. **PSALM 114:9**

Hang the poster in your family room or one of the hallways.

Some things to talk about and do at home:

» What do you think makes a story good?
» Did a story or a book ever make you want to live differently?
» What is your favorite part of the Bible? Who do you like in that story? Are they like you?
» Write your own family psalm of praise or thanksgiving.

ACTIVITY

Blessing Cup

MOMS AND DADS: *Talk with your family.*

In his First Letter to the Corinthians, St. Paul says: "The cup of blessing that we bless, is it not a participation in the blood of Christ? The bread that we break, is it not a participation in the body of Christ?" (1 Corinthians 10:16).

A blessing cup is a reminder of the cup Jesus used at the Last Supper. Our prayers—our lives—are connected to Jesus' life, to the cup of the Last Supper.

At the Last Supper, Jesus prayed for all of us: "Father God, I pray for them…for the ones you have given me, because they are yours."

We, too, pray for others, especially during the General Intercessions at Mass. These prayers at Mass fall into four categories:

- **The needs of the Church:** the pope, the local bishop, all bishops and pastors of the Church, the Church's ministers, the missions, etc.
- **Public authorities and the world:** peace and justice, government officials, an end to war, etc.
- **Those in need:** the unemployed, the sick, those suffering injustices, etc.
- **The local community:** those who are to be baptized, confirmed, or married; First Communicants, etc.

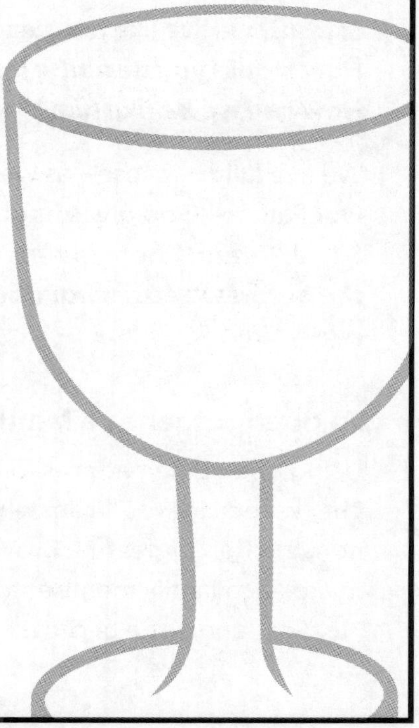

Take a few minutes to decorate your blessing cup, using stickers, yarn, ribbon, markers, etc.

Talk together about the people/situations you want to pray for; write on small pieces of paper; place them in the cup.

When you get home, place the cup on your dinner table. Each time you gather for a meal, take out one intention and especially remember that intention in your family prayer throughout the meal and your day. (You can also add new intentions to your blessing cup at any time.)

ACTIVITY

Our Daily Bread

PARENTS: *Talk about these points with your family.*

Even though we might not receive Communion each day, Jesus is with us each day.
Can you tell us about a time you knew Jesus was with you last week?

We need Jesus every day.
What do you need from Jesus?

Because God gives us everything we need each day, we are grateful.
Think about yesterday; what are you grateful for?

Because we're baptized and are followers of Jesus, we live like Jesus each day.
How would you describe Jesus?
How can we be like him?

We live fully because—as we pray in the Our Father—God gives us our daily bread.
Since "bread" here means more than just the bread we eat, what does God give us every day?

To do together as a family

Using one of the patterns for a "loaf of bread," cut "several loaves" from white or brown construction paper or a brown grocery bag. Invite each family member to take one of the "loaves" and write or draw a prayer. Your prayer might be about one of these three things:

- *Things you need and want to ask God for*
- *Things you have received and want to thank God for*
- *Something you did (are doing) to live like Jesus (and ask God's help to keep on living like Jesus)*

After each person has written or drawn their prayer, take turns showing and telling the others about it. After each one, everyone responds:
Give us this day our daily bread.

To continue at home:

» Take home your prayers as well as all the blank "loaves of bread."

» On your kitchen table, place a breadbasket or bread plate.

» Put the bread shapes and pencils beside the basket.

» Every evening (or once a week), invite family members to take a bread shape and write or draw a simple prayer.

» Share them with each other.

» After each one, everyone responds: Give us this day our daily bread.

» Place the "loaves" with prayers in the breadbasket.

OUR DAILY BREAD

Directions for leader: *Make several copies of these loaves of bread on thick card stock so that the families can use them as patterns for tracing their "loaves of bread" on construction paper or paper bags.*

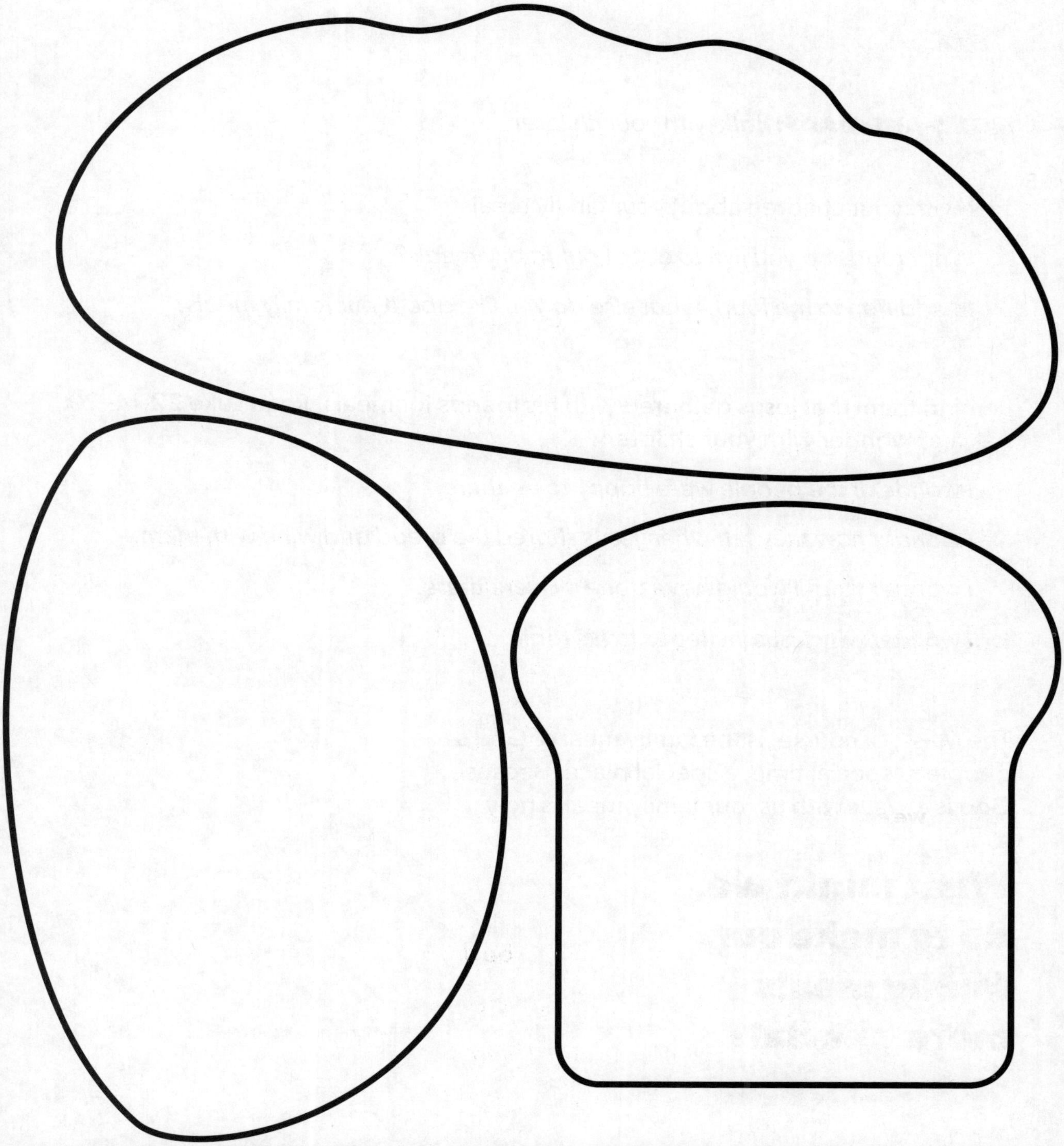

ACTIVITY

We Gather for Meals

MOMS AND DADS: *Talk with your children.*

Talk with your children about your family meals:

What foods do you like to eat at our family meals?

In addition to the food, what else do you like about our family meals?

Remind them that Jesus gathered with his friends for meals. Read Luke 22:14–20. Ask and wonder with your children:

I wonder if the people were happy to be there.

I wonder how they felt when Jesus shared the bread and wine with them.

I wonder what I would have done if I were there.

I wonder why Jesus invites us to his table.

The Mass, of course, is the family meal of God's people, a special time, a special place. Because God is always with us, our family meal is holy too.

What might we do to make our family meals more special?

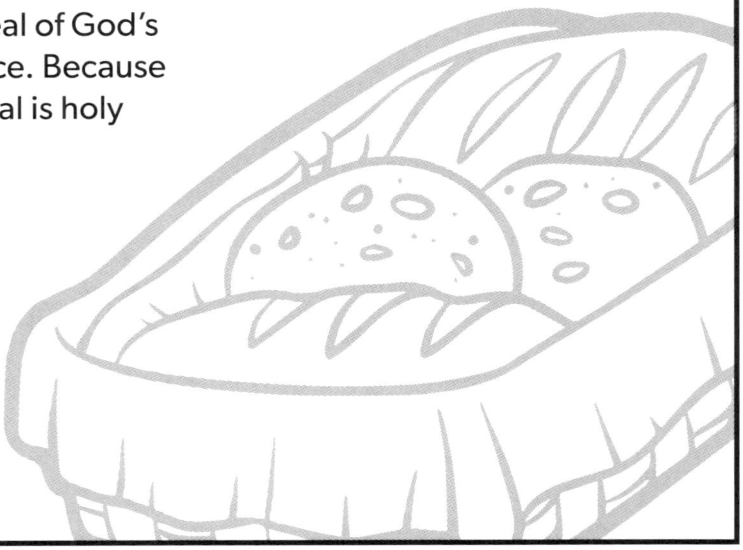

WE GATHER FOR MEALS

As a family, decide on three things you are going to do for your family meals. Write them on your Promise Card below. (Then take it home and place it on your refrigerator.) Some things you might consider:

- Invite each person to mention one thing from the day for which they are grateful.
- Turn off the TVs (and cell phones) and don't start eating until everyone is present.
- Have some special meals: an inside picnic, an "everyone has part of the preparation" dinner, a breakfast when dinnertimes are busy, ethnic dinners, dinnertimes to celebrate special events (first snowfall, TGIF, first tooth out, etc.).
- Hold one conversation at a time.
- Create a weekly dinner ritual when a friend of a family member is invited to dinner or to dessert.
- Include everyone in the meal preparation and in the decision about what foods will be offered for dinner.
- Give thanks—to God and to the cook.
- When a family meal is simply impossible, think about a late-night chocolate milk or hot cocoa moment where everyone can spend a few minutes *catching up or sharing a simple moment from the day.*

Our Family's Promises to each other for our family meals

+ ____________________________

+ ____________________________

+ ____________________________

ACTIVITY

The Eucharist Is about Making Peace

MOMS AND DADS: *Talk with your family about:*

- Often we pray the Our Father at home; we pray it, too, during the Mass.
- One of the things we pray is: "forgive us our trespasses as we forgive those who trespass against us." What are we asking for? What are we promising?
- Shortly after the Our Father, we share a sign of peace (remembering the words that Jesus said to his disciples after the resurrection).
- In these two places (and others), we're reminded that we're called to be peacemakers.

Make placemats that you can use at home that tell about peace. You might want to use words and pictures to show:

- What peace looks like.
- How you are a peacemaker.
- Your best memory of peacefulness within your home.
- Something we could do to have more peace among us.
- How we can bring peace to the world around us.
- What the sign of peace at Mass means to you at Mass.
- Why you think the Church asks us to share the sign of peace.

Things to talk about and do at home:

» Would you say that our home is a peaceful one?

» Are there things we could do to have more peace among us?

» Talk about the many ingredients needed for a successful recipe. What are the needed ingredients for a recipe for family peace? What are the needed ingredients for a recipe for world peace?

» Read through the prayers of the Mass in a missalette. Notice how many times we pray about "God's mercy," "forgiveness," and "reconciling."

ACTIVITY

We Gather to Give Thanks

MOMS AND DADS: *Talk with your family about the following:*

- At every Mass, the priest, praying for himself and all of us, says: "It is truly right and just, our duty and our salvation, always and everywhere to give you thanks, Lord, holy Father, almighty and eternal God."
- If we asked ten people why they go to Mass, we would probably have ten different answers (and they might all be right).
- One major reason is: in the midst of all we've been given by our loving God, all we can do is say "thank you."
- The word **eucharist** comes from a Greek word that means "thanksgiving." We gather, as God's people, to give thanks.

Let's think of some things for which we are thankful:

On the construction paper, write a word down the left-hand side of the paper. The word could be your last name, Eucharist, or thanksgiving, or all your first names combined as one. After each letter, write or draw things for which you are thankful that begin with that letter.

For example: **C — cake, caring, campfires, candy, cats, church, chocolate**

Take your paper home, placing it in your kitchen or near your bedrooms as a reminder of things to be thankful for at mealtime and/or bedtime.

Things to talk about and do at home:

» Make and send a thank-you card to someone who is an important person to your family.

» Compose an "I love you because…" list for everyone in the family, and attach it to your refrigerator.

» On the way to Mass each Sunday, talk about the things that happened during the past week for which each person is grateful. Think about your gratitude for them during Eucharist.

» Begin a family journal of thanks. Each night before bedtime, have everyone write or draw something from the day for which they are grateful.

» Choose one person in the family for each day. Invite everyone to say what that person did—on their day—that they would like to thank God for.

ACTIVITY

The Eucharist Commits Us to Action; to Be the Body of Christ

MOMS AND DADS: *Talk with your family about the following:*

At the Last Supper, Jesus washed the disciples' feet to remind us that we are called to serve others. JOHN 13:13–14

Jesus said to us: "Whatever you do for one of these least sisters or brothers of mine, you do for me." MATTHEW 25:40

The Catechism of the Catholic Church reminds us that celebrating Eucharist commits us to the poor and those in need (CCC #1397).

How do we—or could we—care about others, especially those in need?

The attached handout has some ideas.

- Cut the strips apart, adding three of your ideas onto the three blank links.
- Choose six that your family would like to do in the next six months.
- Make these links into a paper chain to take home as a reminder of your actions for others, of how you will be the body of Christ to others.

Offer to help a neighbor with a job that they have to do.
As a family, visit a shut-in.
Give something away to someone in need.
Do something for someone without them knowing it.
Do you know someone who is elderly, lonely, grieving? Think of something your family could do: pay a visit; bring some baked goods; invite them for a meal.
Find out who in your parish is sick, and offer to visit them or bring them food.
Adopt an elderly person in your neighborhood or parish.
Make bread or muffins and take them to a homeless shelter. Discuss beforehand what to expect. Stay, eat and visit with the people.
Fix a meal for a neighbor who is lonely.
Begin a custom that when you purchase certain things, your family will purchase two: one for your family and one for the needy.

ACTIVITY

My Reflections on Eucharist

PARENTS: *You will probably not be able to complete this activity in our short twenty minutes. But use this time to begin your reflections and generate ideas together as a family (and then it can be completed at home).*

Talk together as a family:

- We often use images/pictures/symbols to express things that are important to us (wedding ring, American flag, etc.).

  What images/symbols tell us about God's love for us?

  What images/symbols tell us about the Eucharist?

- We're going to help you (our First Communicant) make a banner that we can use at home, especially on the day of your First Communion, to tell others your ideas about God's love, about the Eucharist.

- The banner kit contains some patterns for symbols. Which ones tell you about God's love, the Eucharist? (You can think of and draw your own too!)

- Begin to choose your symbols and design your banner.

ACTIVITY

The Gift of the Holy Spirit

(FOR PARISHES THAT CELEBRATE THE RESTORED ORDER OF THE SACRAMENTS)

MOMS AND DADS: *Talk with your family about the following.*

When we were baptized we received the gift of God, the Holy Spirit.

This gift given at baptism is sealed in the sacrament of confirmation—it is deepened and made stronger.

The Holy Spirit works with us and for us in many ways.

One by one, have a family member take one of the slips of paper out of the box (bag or bowl).

As you read it together, talk about what the Holy Spirit does for us.

Because of all these things that the Holy Spirit does for us, the church uses many different symbols/images for the Holy Spirit: wind, breath, fire, a dove, a seal, water, cloud, light, anointing with oil.

Which one do you like?

Can you think of another one?

Using the clay, each person fashions a symbol of the Holy Spirit. It can be one that the Church uses or a new one that helps you to think about the Holy Spirit.

GIFT OF THE HOLY SPIRIT ACTIVITY

Directions for leader: *Cut these apart and place in a box, a bowl, or a bag. Have enough boxes (bowls or bags) for the number of families who will be in this activity center at any given time.*

The Holy Spirit is always with us.

We are never alone. God loves us so much that God the Holy Spirit is with us continually–living with us. When we need help he is never far away but always right with us, waiting for us to call on him for help.

The Holy Spirit is the Comforter.
When we need comfort or when we want to comfort others, the Holy Spirit is with us.

The Holy Spirit encourages us.
When we're worried or not sure what to do, the Holy Spirit is always there.

The Holy Spirit is our Helper.
When we need help, we can stop to listen or feel what the Spirit is saying in our hearts.

The Holy Spirit is like precious oil that strengthens us to do God's work. 1 SAMUEL 16:13

The Holy Spirit guides us.
The Holy Spirit guides us and helps us when we need to make important choices. Sometimes we can feel the Spirit moving us in our hearts, just like we can feel the wind against our bodies. The Holy Spirit guides our feelings and thoughts before we do something.

The Holy Spirit helps us to be brave when we are scared.
2 TIMOTHY 1:7

ACTIVITY

Closing Activity

Talk with your families, using explanations such as:

- *We've talked about several things about God's gift of Eucharist to us today. There's always more to learn and appreciate!*
- *As we end today, let's remember some important realities about Eucharist as we make a mobile of reminders (for our homes).*

Using the paper symbols (from the handout for this activity):

HOLD THE TWO GIFT BOXES IN YOUR HANDS.

- We receive presents lots of time. (Sometimes they're presents we can't see.)
- ***Moms and dads:*** tell your child about a gift he/she has given you.
- ***Boys and girls:*** tell your mom and dad about a gift they have given you in the past or are giving you right now or give you all the time.
- The gift boxes in your hands remind us of our Sunday celebration:
  - We give gifts to God.
  - God gives a gift to us.
- As you attach these two gift boxes to your mobile (hanger) with yarn or ribbon, talk together about:
  - Do you remember some of the gifts we mentioned in our opening activity today that you bring and give to God during Mass?
  - What gift does God give to us?
- Before you hang this up at home, you might want to write some of the gifts on each one.

CHILD PRAYING SYMBOL

- Did you know that there are all kinds of ways of praying?
- Sometimes we group all our prayers into four ways of praying: praise, thanks, asking, sorrow.
- Lots of saints have told us that the most important way we pray is to say thank you.
- Talk with your family: when you pray at home, what are some of the things you say "thank you" to God for?
- As you tie this symbol on to your mobile, talk about: what are some new things you might say "thank you" to God for?

WHEAT AND GRAPES SYMBOL

- Wheat grows. We make it into flour. What are some things we make out of flour?
- Grapes grow. What do we use grapes to make?
- Bread and wine: ordinary foods we find all over the world.
- That's probably why Jesus used them:
    - » *They are found all over the world: Jesus is for everyone.*
    - » *Ordinary food reminds us that's where Jesus is—in all the ordinary things that happen to us. Not only at church, although that time is very important. But Jesus is with us everywhere—in all the ordinary things.*
- As you put the wheat and grapes on your mobile, tell each other about a time when you felt Jesus with you.

PATEN WITH HOST AND CHALICE SYMBOL

- We receive Communion, which is Jesus—Jesus' life.
- What's your favorite food?
- Has your mom ever said to you something like, "If you eat another piece of pizza, you're going to look like a pizza?"
- That's sort of like what Communion is all about.
    - » *We receive Jesus.*
    - » *Jesus said, "This is my Body. Take and eat."*
    - » *We receive Jesus so that we can be like him.*
    - » *People can look at us and say, "They're just like Jesus. That's just what Jesus would do."*
    - » *At times that is hard to do—to be like Jesus.*
    - » *Receiving Jesus every week in Communion helps us to do that. We receive Jesus' love, strength, courage to be like Jesus.*
- As you place this on your mobile, don't talk to each other this time. Just think quietly about how you act like Jesus. Tell Jesus how much you want to receive him every week.

CHURCH BUILDING WITH PEOPLE COMING OUT SYMBOL

- "Mass" means "you are sent."
- The Eucharist never ends. At the conclusion of Mass, the priest (or deacon) sends us to continue living the Eucharist: "Go and announce the Gospel of the Lord" or "Go in peace, glorifying the Lord by your life."
- As you place this symbol on your mobile, talk together: what do we do to spread God's love during the week—not just in our family (as important as that is), but by how we serve and help other people beyond our family?

CLOSING ACTIVITY

ACTIVITY

Closing Prayer

Invite the children to stand and place their hands in blessing on their moms and dads (heads or shoulders). Invite them to pray in their hearts as you pray aloud:

Loving God, thank you for the parents you gave us. We ask that you bless them and always surround them with your love. Bless them with your care because they always care for us. Bless them with your faithfulness for they are always faithful to us, always there for us. We ask this blessing—as we trace the Sign of the Cross on their foreheads—in the name of the Father, and of the Son, and of the Holy Spirit. Amen.

Invite the parents to place their hands in blessing on their child(ren). Invite them to pray in their hearts as you pray aloud:

Ever-Present God, you know how much we love our children, because you, too, are a parent. We are all your daughters and sons.
We are glad that you gave us some of your special children to be our children.
Bless them with your peace—as we make peace and share forgiveness at home.
Bless them with your protection—as we protect them with safety and good health.
Bless them with your gentleness—as we teach them about respect for all creation.
Bless them with your joy and simplicity—as we share happy times of family love with them.
We ask this in your name as we, once again, sign them with the Sign of the Cross as we did at their baptism. Amen.